sauces

sauces

classic & contemporary sauces

This edition published in 2010
LOVE FOOD is an imprint of Parragon Books Ltd

Parragon
Queen Street House
4 Queen Street
Bath BA1 1HE, UK

ISBN: 978-1-4454-0701-2

Printed in China

Produced by the Bridgewater Book Company Ltd
Design concept by Fiona Roberts

Notes for the Reader
This book uses imperial, metric, and US cup measurements. Follow the same units of measurement throughout; do not mix imperial and metric. All spoon measurements are level: teaspoons are assumed to be 5 ml, and tablespoons are assumed to be 15 ml. Unless otherwise stated, milk is assumed to be whole, eggs and individual vegetables such as potatoes are medium, and pepper is freshly ground black pepper.

The times given are an approximate guide only. Preparation times differ according to the techniques used by different people and the cooking times may also vary from those given as a result of the type of oven used. Optional ingredients, variations or serving suggestions have not been included in the calculations.

Recipes using raw or very lightly cooked eggs should be avoided by infants, the elderly, pregnant women, convalescents, and anyone with a chronic condition. Pregnant and breastfeeding women are advised to avoid eating peanuts and peanut products. Sufferers from nut allergies should be aware that some of the ready-prepared ingredients used in the recipes in this book may contain nuts. Always check the packaging before use.

Introduction

It is said that one of the things that distinguishes a good cook from a great one is the quality of their sauces and there is no doubt that a well-made complementary sauce can transform an ordinary meal into something exceptional. It can add creamy richness, enhance the flavor of a dish's main ingredient, balance textures, and often adds a touch of elegance to the presentation.

In this book, the section of recipes classified as dips includes delicious condiments that can be served with crudités, pita bread, tortilla chips, and breadsticks, to make a single, stand-alone dish. Many of these, however, can also serve as wonderful sauces. Try Guacamole with broiled steak, or Pico de Gallo Salsa with barbecued chicken, for example.

Three further sections are devoted exclusively to sauces in the conventional sense. Savory Sauces includes many world-wide favorites that can make or break a recipe. Just try to imagine succulent steamed asparagus without Hollandaise.

Essential Recipes provides a collection of sauces and salad dressings that form the core of a cook's repertoire. These range from traditional standbys such as Mayonnaise to more contemporary accompaniments such as Apricot Sauce and Mango Chutney. Finally, Sweet Sauces offers a host of alternatives to the ubiquitous ice cream, including, of course, some special treats for chocoholics.

Whether you serve them with a colorful platter of raw vegetables or a basket of sesame seed crackers, dips are the key to easy entertaining. The recipes within this chapter use ingredients as varied as avocados, beans, red bell peppers, and coconut to guarantee that there will be something to suit every taste and every budget. This is an international collection with dishes from countries as far apart as Mexico, Indonesia, Greece, and India and flavors ranging from hot and spicy to cool and refreshing and from rich and creamy to sharp and tantalizing. As they are all so easy to make you can serve a whole array of dips as part of a party buffet table. Equally, two or three contrasting dips would make an unusual appetizer for a dinner party and get the taste buds tingling. You can even serve individual dips as a colorful and attractive accompaniment to liven up a simple main course.

DELICIOUS DIPS

SERVES 4

2 large, ripe avocados

juice of 1 lime, or to taste

2 tsp olive oil

½ onion, finely chopped

1 fresh green chili, such as poblano, seeded and finely chopped

1 garlic clove, crushed

¼ tsp ground cumin

1 tbsp chopped fresh cilantro

salt and pepper

chopped fresh cilantro, to garnish (optional)

Guacamole

A good result always depends on using quality, ripe avocados. Mashing rather than puréeing gives control over the texture.

• Cut the avocados in half lengthwise and twist the 2 halves in opposite directions to separate. Stab the pit with the point of a sharp knife and lift out.

• Peel, then coarsely chop the avocado halves and place in a non-metallic bowl. Squeeze over the lime juice and add the oil.

• Mash the avocados with a fork until the desired consistency—either chunky or smooth. Blend in the onion, chili, garlic, cumin, and chopped cilantro, then season to taste with salt and pepper.

• Transfer to a serving dish and serve at once, to avoid discoloration, sprinkled with extra chopped cilantro, if liked.

SERVES 8

8 oz/225 g dried chickpeas, covered with water and soaked overnight
juice of 2 large lemons
2/3 cup sesame seed paste (tahini)
2 garlic cloves, crushed
4 tbsp extra-virgin olive oil
small pinch of ground cumin
salt and pepper
1 tsp paprika
chopped flat-leaf parsley, to garnish
pita bread, to serve

Chickpea and Sesame Dip

This is a favorite Greek dish that is found on most meze tables. It is best made with dried, rather than canned, chickpeas. It is simple to make, especially if prepared in a food processor.

• Drain the chickpeas, put in a saucepan, and cover with cold water. Bring to the boil then simmer for about 2 hours, or until very tender.

• Drain the chickpeas, reserving a little of the liquid, and put in a food processor, reserving a few to garnish. Blend the chickpeas until smooth, gradually adding the lemon juice and enough reserved liquid to form a smooth, thick purée. Add the sesame seed paste, garlic, 3 tablespoons of the olive oil and the cumin and blend until smooth. Season with salt and pepper.

• Turn the mixture into a shallow serving dish and chill in the fridge for 2–3 hours before serving. To serve, mix the reserved olive oil with the paprika and drizzle over the top of the dish. Sprinkle with the parsley and the reserved chickpeas. Accompany with warm pita bread.

SERVES 4

2 bulbs garlic
6 tbsp olive oil
1 small onion, finely chopped
2 tbsp lemon juice
3 tbsp sesame seed paste (tahini)
2 tbsp chopped parsley
salt and pepper
fresh vegetable crudités, French bread, or warmed pocket breads, to serve

Heavenly Garlic Dip

If you come across smoked garlic, use it in this recipe—it tastes wonderful. There is no need to roast the smoked garlic, so omit the first step.

• Separate the bulbs of garlic into individual cloves. Place them on a cookie sheet and roast in a preheated oven, 400°F/200°C, for 8–10 minutes. Set them aside to cool for a few minutes.
• When they are cool enough to handle, peel the garlic cloves and then chop them finely.
• Heat the olive oil in a pan or skillet and add the garlic and onion. Sauté over low heat, stirring occasionally, for 8–10 minutes, or until soft. Remove the pan from the heat.
• Mix in the lemon juice, sesame seed paste, and parsley. Season to taste with salt and pepper. Transfer the dip to a small heatproof bowl.
• Serve with fresh vegetable crudités, or with chunks of French bread or warm pocket breads.

SERVES 4

1 small cucumber

½ pint/300 ml authentic Greek yogurt

1 large garlic clove, crushed

1 tbsp chopped fresh mint or dill

salt and pepper

warm pita bread, to serve

Cucumber and Yogurt Dip

This wonderfully cooling combination of yogurt, cucumber, and mint is especially good as an accompaniment to very spicy curries. If you are taken by surprise with the heat of a curry, don't reach for a glass of water, try this soothing dip!

• Peel then coarsely grate the cucumber. Put in a sieve and squeeze out as much of the water as possible. Put the cucumber into a bowl.

• Add the yogurt, garlic, and chopped mint (reserve a little as a garnish, if desired) to the cucumber and season with pepper. Mix well together and chill in the fridge for about 2 hours before serving.

• To serve, stir the cucumber and yogurt dip and transfer to a serving bowl. Sprinkle with salt and accompany with warmed pita bread.

SERVES 4

3 large garlic cloves, finely chopped
2 egg yolks
1 cup extra-virgin olive oil
1 tbsp lemon juice
1 tbsp lime juice
1 tbsp Dijon mustard
1 tbsp chopped fresh tarragon
salt and pepper
1 fresh tarragon sprig, to garnish

Aïoli

It is essential to add oil slowly to the egg yolks to prevent them from curdling until between one-third and one-half has been fully incorporated. If the mixture does curdle, add it, a little at a time, to another egg yolk, whisking constantly, then return it to the food processor, and gradually add the remaining oil with the motor running.

• Ensure that all the ingredients are at room temperature. Place the garlic and egg yolks in a food processor and process until well blended. With the motor running, pour in the oil, teaspoon by teaspoon, through the feeder tube until the mixture starts to thicken, then pour in the remaining oil in a thin stream until a thick mayonnaise forms.
• Add the lemon and lime juices, mustard, and tarragon and season to taste with salt and pepper. Blend until smooth, then transfer to a nonmetallic bowl. Garnish with a tarragon sprig.
• Cover with plastic wrap and let chill until required.

SERVES 6

8 oz/225 g smoked cod roe or fresh gray mullet roe
1 small onion, quartered
¼ cup fresh white breadcrumbs
1 large garlic clove, crushed
grated rind and juice of 1 large lemon
⅓ cup extra-virgin olive oil
6 tbsp hot water
pepper
black Greek olives, to garnish
capers
chopped flat-leaf parsley
crackers, potato chips or pita bread, to serve

Smoked Cod Roe Dip

This dish was traditionally made with salted mullet roe which is the true tarama and from which it derives its Greek name *taramasalata*. Nowadays, however, it is usually made with smoked cod roe that is more readily available.

• Remove the skin from the fish roe. Put the onion in a food processor and chop finely. Add the cod roe in small pieces and blend until smooth. Add the breadcrumbs, garlic, lemon rind and juice, and mix well together.

• With the machine running, very slowly pour in the oil. When all the oil has been added, blend in the water. Season with pepper.

• Turn the mixture into a serving bowl and chill in the fridge for at least 1 hour before serving. Serve garnished with olives, capers, and chopped parsley and accompany with crackers, chips or pita bread.

SERVES 6–8

2 large eggplants
2 red bell peppers
4 tbsp Spanish olive oil
2 garlic cloves, roughly chopped
grated rind and juice of ½ lemon
1 tbsp chopped fresh coriander
½–1 tsp paprika
salt and pepper
fresh chopped cilantro, to garnish
bread or toast, to serve

Eggplant and Bell Pepper Dip

As a variation, instead of cooking the eggplants and bell peppers in the oven, they can be cooked under a preheated broiler until the skins are charred all over. They do, however, need to be turned frequently and will take about 10 minutes.

- Preheat the oven to 375°F/190°C. Prick the skins of the eggplants and bell peppers all over with a fork and brush with 1 tablespoon of the olive oil. Place on a baking sheet and bake in the preheated oven for 45 minutes, or until the skins are beginning to turn black, the flesh of the eggplant is very soft, and the bell peppers are deflated.
- Place the cooked vegetables in a bowl and cover tightly with a clean, damp dish towel. Alternatively, place the vegetables in a plastic bag and let stand for about 15 minutes, or until cool enough to handle.
- When the vegetables have cooled, cut the eggplants in half lengthwise, carefully scoop out the flesh and discard the skin. Cut the eggplant flesh into large chunks. Remove and discard the stem, core, and seeds from the bell peppers and cut the flesh into large pieces.
- Heat the remaining olive oil in a skillet. Add the eggplant and bell pepper and cook for 5 minutes. Add the garlic and cook for 30 seconds.
- Turn the contents of the skillet onto paper towels to drain, then transfer to a food processor. Add the lemon rind and juice, the chopped cilantro, the paprika, and salt and pepper to taste, then process until a speckled purée is formed.
- Transfer the eggplant and bell pepper dip to a serving bowl. Serve warm or at room temperature. Alternatively, let cool for 30 minutes, then let chill in the refrigerator for at least 1 hour, then serve cold. Garnish with cilantro sprigs and accompany with thick slices of bread or toast for dipping.

MAKES ABOUT 1½ CUPS

3½ oz/100 g tamarind pulp, chopped, or paste*

2 cups water

½ Thai chili, or to taste, seeded and chopped

generous ¼ cup brown sugar, or to taste

½ tsp salt

*ready-to-use tamarind paste should be available from your local store

Tamarind Chutney

There isn't any mistaking the fresh, sour taste of tamarind: it adds a distinctive flavor to many dishes, especially those from Southern India. More like a sauce than a chutney, this sweet-and-sour tasting mixture is excellent served with vegetable samosas.

- Put the tamarind and water in a heavy-bottom pan over high heat and bring to a boil. Reduce the heat to the lowest setting and simmer for 25 minutes, stirring occasionally to break up the tamarind pulp, or until tender.
- Tip the tamarind pulp into a strainer and use a wooden spoon to push the pulp into the rinsed-out pan.
- Stir in the chili, sugar, and salt and continue simmering for an additional 10 minutes or until the desired consistency is reached. Let cool slightly, then stir in extra sugar or salt, to taste.
- Let cool completely, then cover tightly and chill for up to 3 days, or freeze.

SERVES 4

2 cups toasted pumpkin seeds
4 cups vegetable bouillon
several pinches of ground cloves
8–10 tomatillos, diced, or use 1 cup mild tomatillo salsa
½ onion, chopped
½ fresh green chili, seeded and diced
3 garlic cloves, chopped
½ tsp fresh thyme leaves
½ tsp fresh marjoram leaves
3 tbsp vegetable oil
3 bay leaves
4 tbsp chopped fresh cilantro
salt and pepper
green bell pepper, to garnish
tortilla chips, to serve

Mole Verde

As a variation, make a tamale dough and poach in the mole as dumplings, making a filling snack.

- Grind the toasted pumpkin seeds in a food processor. Add half the vegetable bouillon, the cloves, tomatillos, onion, chili, garlic, thyme, and marjoram and blend to a purée.
- Heat the oil in a heavy skillet and add the puréed pumpkin seed mixture and the bay leaves. Cook over medium–high heat for about 5 minutes until the mixture has thickened.
- Remove from the heat and add the rest of the bouillon and the cilantro. Cook until it thickens, then remove from the heat.
- Remove the bay leaves and process until smooth again. Add salt and pepper to taste.
- Transfer to a bowl, garnish with bell pepper strips and serve with tortilla chips.

MAKES ABOUT 1⅓ CUPS

1–2 fresh green chilies, seeded or not, to taste, and finely chopped

1 small Thai chili, seeded or not, to taste, and finely chopped

1 tbsp white wine or cider vinegar

2 onions, finely chopped

2 tbsp fresh lemon juice

1 tbsp sugar

3 tbsp chopped fresh cilantro, mint, or parsley, or a combination of herbs

salt

chili flower, to garnish

Chili and Onion Chutney

For those who really like spicy hot food, this fresh chutney packs quite a punch. It's hot, zingy and can bring tears to your eyes if you don't deseed the chilies. Indians will include the chili seeds and serve this at all meals.

- Put the chilies in a small nonmetallic bowl with the vinegar, stir around, and then drain. Return the chilies to the bowl and stir in the onions, lemon juice, sugar, and herbs, then add salt to taste.
- Let stand at room temperature or cover and chill for 15 minutes. Garnish with the chili flower before serving.

MAKES ABOUT 1½ CUPS

- 1½ tbsp lemon juice
- 1½ tbsp water
- 3 oz/85 g fresh cilantro leaves and stems, coarsely chopped
- 2 tbsp chopped fresh coconut
- 1 small shallot, very finely chopped
- ¼-inch/5-mm piece fresh gingerroot, chopped
- 1 fresh green chili, seeded and chopped
- ½ tsp sugar
- ½ tsp salt
- pinch of pepper

Cilantro Chutney

This is an example of one of the uncooked, fresh tasting chutneys that are served with every meal or snack throughout the day in India.

• Put the lemon juice and water in a small food processor, add half the cilantro, and process until it is blended and a slushy paste forms. Gradually add the remaining cilantro and process until it is all blended, scraping down the sides of the processor, if necessary. If you don't have a processor that will cope with this small amount, use a pestle and mortar, adding the cilantro in small amounts.

• Add the remaining ingredients and continue processing until they are all finely chopped and blended. Taste and adjust any of the seasonings, if you like. Transfer to a nonmetallic bowl, cover, and chill for up to 3 days before serving.

SERVES 6

9 oz/250 g yellow split peas

2 small onions, 1 chopped coarsely and 1 chopped very finely

1 garlic clove, chopped coarsely

6 tbsp extra-virgin olive oil

1 tbsp chopped fresh oregano

salt and pepper

savory crackers, to serve

Split Pea Dip

This is a very popular Greek meze dish. It is simple to make but even easier if prepared in a food processor.

• Rinse the split peas under cold running water. Put in a saucepan and add the coarsely chopped onion, the garlic, and plenty of cold water. Bring to the boil then simmer for about 45 minutes, until very tender.

• Drain the split peas, reserving a little of the cooking liquid, and put in a food processor. Add 5 tablespoons of the olive oil and blend until smooth. If the mixture seems too dry, add enough of the reserved liquid to form a smooth, thick purée. Add the oregano and season with salt and pepper.

• Turn the mixture into a serving bowl and sprinkle with the finely chopped onion and extra oregano if desired. Drizzle over the remaining olive oil. Serve warm or cold with savory crackers.

SERVES 6

2 large eggplants

1/4 cup extra-virgin olive oil

juice of 1/2 lemon

2/3 cup authentic Greek yogurt

2 garlic cloves, crushed

pinch of ground cumin

salt and pepper

chopped fresh flat-leaf parsley, to garnish

strips of orange and green bell pepper, to serve

Eggplant and Garlic Dip

If you prefer your garlic with a mellower flavor, add it to the skillet with the eggplant flesh and tip them both into the food processor after 5 minutes. Cooking reduces the sharpness of garlic.

• Prick the skins of the eggplants with a fork and put on a baking sheet. Bake in a preheated oven, 370°F/190°C, for 45 minutes, or until very soft. Leave to cool slightly then cut the eggplants in half lengthwise and scoop out the flesh.

• Heat the oil in a large, heavy skillet, add the eggplant flesh and fry for 5 minutes. Put the eggplant mixture into a food processor, add the lemon juice, and blend until smooth. Gradually add the yogurt then the garlic and cumin. Season with salt and pepper.

• Turn the mixture into a serving bowl and chill in the fridge for at least 1 hour. Garnish with chopped parsley and serve with raw bell pepper strips or sesame crackers.

SERVES 4

MINT RAITA

- scant 1 cup low-fat unsweetened yogurt
- 1/4 cup water
- 1 small onion, finely chopped
- 1/2 tsp mint sauce
- 1/2 tsp salt
- 3 fresh mint leaves, to garnish

CUCUMBER RAITA

- 1/2 lb/225 g cucumber
- 1 medium onion
- 1/2 tsp salt
- 1/2 tsp mint sauce
- 1 1/4 cups low-fat unsweetened yogurt
- 2/3 cup water
- fresh mint leaves, to garnish

EGGPLANT RAITA

- 1 medium eggplant
- 1 tsp salt
- 1 small onion, finely chopped
- 2 fresh green chilies, seeded and finely chopped
- scant 1 cup low-fat unsweetened yogurt
- 3 tbsp water

Raitas

Raitas are easy to prepare, very versatile, and have a wonderful cooling effect which will be appreciated if you are serving with hot, spicy dishes.

• To make the mint raita, place the yogurt in a bowl and whisk with a fork. Gradually whisk in the water. Add the onion, mint sauce, and salt and blend together. Garnish with mint leaves.

• To make the cucumber raita, peel and slice the cucumber. Chop the onion finely. Place the cucumber and onion in a large bowl, then add the salt and the mint sauce. Add the yogurt and the water, place the mixture in a blender, and blend well. Serve garnished with mint leaves.

• To make the eggplant raita, remove the top end of the eggplant and chop the rest into small pieces. Boil in a pan of water until soft, then drain and mash. Add the salt, onion, and green chilies to the eggplant, mixing well. Whisk the yogurt with the water, add to the mixture, and mix thoroughly.

SERVES 6–8

1 large eggplant, about 14 oz/400 g
olive oil
2 scallions, chopped finely
1 large garlic clove, crushed
2 tbsp finely chopped fresh parsley
salt and pepper
smoked sweet Spanish paprika, to garnish
French bread, to serve

Broiled Eggplant Dip

If you are short of time, you can omit sprinkling the eggplant with salt because modern varieties are far less bitter than those of the past. However, salting the flesh also helps to draw out moisture and prevent it from absorbing too much oil during cooking.

• Cut the eggplant into thick slices and sprinkle with salt to draw out any bitterness; set aside for 30 minutes, then rinse and pat dry.

• Heat 4 tablespoons of the oil in a large skillet over medium-high heat. Add the eggplant slices and cook on both sides until soft and starting to brown. Remove from the skillet and set aside to cool. The slices will release the oil again as they cool.

• Heat another tablespoon of oil in the skillet. Add the onions and garlic and cook for 3 minutes until the scallions become soft. Remove from the heat and set aside with the eggplant slices to cool.

• Transfer all the ingredients to a food processor and process just until a coarse purée forms. Transfer to a serving bowl and stir in the parsley. Taste and adjust the seasoning, if necessary. Serve at once, or cover and let chill until 15 minutes before required. Sprinkle with paprika and serve with slices of French bread.

SERVES 4–6

3 large, ripe tomatoes

½ red onion, finely chopped

1 large fresh green chili, such as jalapeño, seeded and finely chopped

2 tbsp chopped fresh cilantro

juice of 1 lime, or to taste

salt and pepper

Pico de Gallo Salsa

This famous salsa's name translates as "rooster's beak", allegedly, because it was traditionally eaten between the thumb and forefinger, pecking-style.

• Halve the tomatoes, then scoop out and discard the seeds, and dice the flesh. Place the flesh in a large, nonmetallic bowl.

• Add the onion, chili, chopped cilantro and lime juice. Season to taste with salt and pepper and stir gently to combine.

• Cover and let chill in the refrigerator for at least 30 minutes to allow the flavors to develop before serving.

MAKES ABOUT 1 CUP

½ fresh coconut, about 4 oz/115 g of meat, or 1¼ cups dry unsweetened coconut

2 fresh green chilies, seeded or not, to taste, and chopped

1-inch/2.5-cm piece fresh gingerroot, peeled and finely chopped

4 tbsp chopped fresh cilantro

2 tbsp lemon juice, or to taste

2 shallots, very finely chopped

poppadoms, to serve

Coconut Sambal

This dish is good served with poppadoms as a snack or with simply grilled fresh seafood.

• If you are using a whole coconut, use a hammer and nail to punch a hole in the "eye" of the coconut, then pour out the water from the inside and reserve. Use the hammer to break the coconut in half, then peel half and chop.

• Put the coconut and chilies in a small food processor and whiz for about 30 seconds until finely chopped. Add the ginger, cilantro, and lemon juice and whiz again.

• If the mixture seems too dry, whiz in about 1 tablespoon coconut water or water. Stir in the shallots and serve at once, or cover and chill until required. This will keep its fresh flavor, covered, in the refrigerator for up to 3 days.

SERVES 6

scant 1 cup dried cannellini beans
1 small garlic clove, crushed
1 bunch of scallions, coarsely chopped
handful of fresh mint leaves
2 tbsp tahini
2 tbsp olive oil
1 tsp ground cumin
1 tsp ground coriander
lemon juice
salt and pepper
fresh mint sprigs, to garnish
fresh vegetable crudités, such as cauliflower florets, carrots, cucumber, radishes, and bell peppers, to serve

Mint and Cannellini Bean Dip

You could make this dip with other kinds of dried bean—white, kidney, and navy beans would work well, but you could also use borlotti, pinto, or flageolets. Soak in cold water and cook as described in the main recipe until tender—some varieties will take longer than others. Do not add salt when boiling any dried beans or they will become tough.

- Put the cannellini beans into a bowl and add sufficient cold water to cover. Set aside to soak for at least 4 hours or overnight.
- Rinse and drain the beans, put them into a large pan, and cover them with cold water. Bring to a boil and boil rapidly for 10 minutes. Reduce the heat, cover, and simmer until tender.
- Drain the beans thoroughly and transfer them to a bowl or food processor. Add the garlic, scallions, mint, tahini, and olive oil. Process the mixture for about 15 seconds or mash well by hand until smooth.
- Scrape the mixture into a bowl, if necessary, and stir in the cumin, coriander, and lemon juice. Season to taste with salt and pepper. Mix thoroughly, cover with plastic wrap, and set aside in a cool place, but not the refrigerator, for 30 minutes to allow the flavors to develop.
- Spoon the dip into individual serving bowls and garnish with sprigs of fresh mint. Place the bowls on plates and surround them with vegetable crudités. Serve at room temperature.

Of the thirteen recipes in this section, some, such as Classic Bolognese Meat Sauce, form an integral part of a dish while others, such as Romesco Sauce, are designed to add that special extra touch. There are sauces for pasta, dipping, coating, pouring, and to all intents and purposes mopping up with bread at the end of the meal because they are far too delicious to leave on the plate. These sauces are based on a wide range of ingredients from meat to seafood and from vegetables to eggs and can be served with an equally extensive choice of dishes. To take just one example, Satay Sauce is great with grilled chicken, pork, beef, shrimp, fish, and vegetable kabobs and is a sensational topping for boiled new potatoes. Master the art of making any of these sauces—it isn't difficult—and you automatically expand your repertoire of appetizers and main course dishes.

SAVORY SAUCES

SERVES 4

2 tbsp olive oil
1 tbsp butter
1 small onion, chopped finely
1 carrot, chopped finely
1 celery stalk, chopped finely
1 cup mushrooms, diced
2 cups ground beef
¼ cup unsmoked bacon or ham, diced
2 chicken livers, chopped
2 tbsp tomato paste
½ cup dry white wine
salt and pepper
½ tsp freshly grated nutmeg
1¼ cups chicken bouillon
½ cup heavy cream
1 lb/450 g dried spaghetti
2 tbsp chopped fresh parsley, to garnish
freshly grated Parmesan, to serve

Classic Bolognese Meat Sauce

In Bologna, the city in northern Italy where this sauce originated, it is simply called *ragù* and is always served with tagliatelle. Nevertheless, spaghetti bolognese has become traditional elsewhere and even though purists may not approve, the sauce goes well with any kind of pasta to which it can cling, even small shapes, such as fusilli, which children find easier to eat and more appealing.

- Heat the oil and butter in a large pan over a medium heat. Add the onion, carrot, celery, and mushrooms to the pan, then cook until soft. Add the beef and bacon to the pan and cook until the beef is evenly browned.
- Stir in the chicken livers and tomato paste and cook for 2–3 minutes. Pour in the wine and season with salt, pepper, and the nutmeg. Add the bouillon. Bring to a boil, then cover and simmer gently over a low heat for 1 hour. Stir in the cream and simmer, uncovered, until reduced.
- Cook the pasta in plenty of boiling salted water until al dente. Drain and transfer to a warm serving dish.
- Pour half the sauce over the pasta. Toss well to mix. Spoon the remaining sauce over the top.
- Garnish with the parsley and serve with Parmesan cheese.

SERVES 4

2 tbsp vegetable or peanut oil

1 tbsp sesame oil

juice of ½ lime

2 skinless, boneless chicken breasts, cut into small cubes

SATAY SAUCE

2 tbsp vegetable or peanut oil

1 small onion, chopped finely

1 small fresh green chili, seeded and chopped

1 garlic clove, chopped finely

½ cup crunchy peanut butter

6-8 tbsp water

juice of ½ lime

Chicken Satay Sauce

These taste great cooked under the broiler, but using the barbecue adds that extra smoky flavor.

• Combine both the oils and the lime juice in a nonmetallic dish. Add the chicken cubes, cover with plastic wrap, and let chill for 1 hour.

• To make the dip, heat the oil in a skillet and sauté the onion, chili, and garlic over low heat, stirring occasionally, for about 5 minutes, until just softened. Add the peanut butter, water, and lime juice and let simmer gently, stirring constantly, until the peanut butter has softened enough to make a dip—you may need to add extra water to make a thinner consistency.

• Meanwhile, drain the chicken cubes and thread them onto 8–12 wooden skewers. Put under a hot broiler or on a barbecue, turning frequently, for about 10 minutes, until cooked and browned. Serve hot with the sauce.

MAKES ABOUT 1 CUP

2 garlic cloves, coarsely chopped

1/4 cup pine nuts

3/4 cup fresh basil leaves

1 tsp coarse salt

1/3 cup freshly grated Parmesan cheese

1/2–2/3 cup extra-virgin olive oil

Pesto Genovese

Pesto was invented in the Italian port of Genoa whose citizens claim to grow the best basil in the world. Nowadays, it is made with a wide variety of different herbs, such as parsley, mint, or arugula, and even sun-dried tomatoes in oil can be substituted for the basil. Try using hazelnuts or walnuts instead of pine nuts for a change of flavor.

- For the Pesto Genovese, put the garlic, pine nuts, basil leaves, and salt into a blender and process to a purée. Add the Parmesan and process briefly again. You can do this by hand using a pestle and mortar.
- Add 1/2 cup of the oil and process again. If the consistency is too thick, add the remaining oil and process again until smooth.

MAKES ABOUT 1¼ CUPS

4 large, ripe tomatoes

16 blanched almonds

3 large garlic cloves, unpeeled and left whole

1 dried sweet chili, such as ñora, soaked for 20 minutes and patted dry

4 dried red chilies, soaked for 20 minutes and patted dry

pinch of sugar

⅔ cup extra-virgin olive oil

about 2 tbsp red wine vinegar

salt and pepper

Romesco Sauce

This tomato sauce is traditionally served with fish and shellfish but is ideal for adding instant flavor to simply cooked chicken, pork or lamb dishes. Authentic recipes are made with dried romesco chilies, which have a sweet and hot flavor. Unfortunately they are quite hard to obtain, so this recipe uses dried ñora chili.

• Place the tomatoes, blanched almonds, and garlic on a baking sheet and roast in a preheated oven, 350°F/180°C, for 20 minutes, but check the almonds after about 7 minutes, because they can burn quickly; remove as soon as they are golden and giving off an aroma.

• Peel the roasted garlic and tomatoes. Put the almonds, garlic, sweet chili, and dried red chilies in a food processor and process until finely chopped. Add the tomatoes and sugar and process again.

• With the motor running, slowly add the olive oil through the feed tube. Add 1½ tablespoons of the vinegar and quickly process. Taste and add extra vinegar, if desired, and salt and pepper to taste.

• Let stand for at least 2 hours, then serve at room temperature. Alternatively, cover and chill for up to 3 days, then bring to room temperature before serving. Stir in any oil that separates before serving.

SERVES 4

1 tbsp olive oil

2 tbsp butter

1 onion, chopped finely

scant 2/3 cup ham, diced

2 garlic cloves, chopped very finely

1 fresh red chili, seeded and finely chopped

1 lb 12 oz/800 g canned chopped tomatoes

salt and pepper

4 cups bucatini or penne pasta

2 tbsp chopped fresh flat-leaf parsley

6 tbsp freshly grated Parmesan

Ham, Tomato, and Chili Sauce

The heat of chilies, measured in Scoville units, varies tremendously, so if you are not sure how hot the ones you have bought are, err on the side of caution. As a general rule, small, pointed chilies are hotter than fatter, round ones, but even pods picked from the same bush can vary. Fully ripe, red chilies have a sweeter flavor than green ones.

• Put the olive oil and 1 tablespoon of the butter in a large skillet over a medium–low heat. Add the onion and cook for 10 minutes, or until soft and golden. Add the ham and cook for 5 minutes, or until lightly browned. Stir in the garlic, chili and tomatoes. Season with a little salt and pepper. Bring to a boil, then simmer over a medium–low heat for 30–40 minutes, or until thickened.

• Cook the pasta in plenty of boiling salted water until al dente. Drain and transfer to a warm serving dish.

• Pour the sauce over the pasta. Add the parsley, Parmesan, and the remaining butter. Toss well to mix, and serve immediately.

SERVES 4

FISHCAKES

- 1 lb/450 g white fish fillets, skinned and cut into cubes
- 1 egg white
- 2 kaffir lime leaves, torn coarsely
- 1 tbsp Green Curry Paste
- 2 oz green beans, chopped finely
- 1 fresh red chili, seeded and chopped finely
- bunch of fresh cilantro, chopped
- vegetable or peanut oil for cooking

DIPPING SAUCE

- generous ½ cup super fine sugar
- ¼ cup white wine vinegar
- 1 small carrot, cut into thin sticks
- 2-inch/5-cm piece cucumber, peeled, seeded, and cut into thin sticks

Fish Cakes and Thai Dipping Sauce

Dipping sauces are hugely popular in Thailand and this one can be served with a wide variety of other tasty morsels, including pancake rolls, deep-fried crab claws, wonton pouches, rice cakes, and miniature meatballs. If you like, you can substitute rice vinegar for the white wine vinegar and add a pinch of chopped fresh or crushed dried chili.

• Put the fish into a food processor with the egg white, lime leaves, and curry paste, and process until smooth. Scrape the mixture into a bowl and stir in the green beans, red chili, and cilantro.

• With dampened hands, shape the mixture into small patties, about 2 inches across. Place them on a large plate in a single layer and let chill for 30 minutes.

• Meanwhile, make the dipping sauce. Put the sugar in a pan with 1½ tablespoons water and the vinegar and heat gently, stirring until the sugar has dissolved. Add the carrot and cucumber, then remove from the heat and let cool.

• Heat the oil in a skillet and cook the fish cakes, in batches, until golden brown on both sides. Drain on paper towels and keep warm while you cook the remaining batches. If desired, reheat the dipping sauce. Serve the fish cakes immediately with warm or cold dipping sauce.

MAKES 1 CUP

10 dried arbol chilies, stems removed

1 cup cider or white wine vinegar

½ tsp salt

Hot Sauce of Dried Chilies

Arbol are dried long hot red chilies, with a dusty heat that is reminiscent of the Mexican Desert. If Arbol chilies are not available, use hot dried chili or chili flakes, such as cayenne.

• Place the chilies in a mortar and crush finely with a pestle.

• Put the vinegar in a pan and add the chilies and salt. Stir to combine, then bring to a boil.

• Remove from the heat and let cool and infuse. Pour into a bowl and serve. The sauce will keep for up to a month, covered, in the refrigerator.

SERVES 4

1 lb/450 g spareribs, cut into bite-size pieces

vegetable or peanut oil, for deep-frying

MARINADE

2 tsp light soy sauce

½ tsp salt

pinch of white pepper

SAUCE

3 tbsp white rice vinegar

2 tbsp sugar

1 tbsp light soy sauce

1 tbsp tomato ketchup

1½ tbsp vegetable or peanut oil

1 green bell pepper, coarsely chopped

1 small onion, coarsely chopped

1 small carrot, finely sliced ½ tsp finely chopped garlic

½ tsp finely chopped ginger

3½ oz/100 g pineapple chunks

Spareribs in a Sweet-and-Sour Sauce

The original sweet-and-sour sauce, on which this version is based, is associated with fish. This sweet-and-sour sauce, incorporating tomato ketchup and pineapple chunks is matched with pork.

• Combine the marinade ingredients in a bowl with the spareribs and marinate for at least 20 minutes.

• Heat enough oil for deep-frying in a wok, deep-fat fryer or large heavy-bottom pan until it reaches 350–375°F/180–190°C, or until a cube of bread browns in 30 seconds. Deep-fry the spareribs for 8 minutes. Drain and set aside.

• To prepare the sauce, first mix together the vinegar, sugar, light soy sauce, and ketchup. Set aside.

• In a preheated wok or deep pan, heat 1 tablespoon of the oil and stir-fry the bell pepper, onion, and carrot for 2 minutes. Remove and set aside.

• In the clean preheated wok or deep pan, heat the remaining oil and stir-fry the garlic and ginger until fragrant. Add the vinegar mixture. Bring back to a boil and add the pineapple chunks. Finally add the spareribs and the bell pepper, onion, and carrot. Stir until warmed through and serve immediately.

SERVES 4

1 lb/450 g tagliatelle or conchiglie

1¼ cups sour cream

2 tsp Dijon mustard

4 large scallions, finely sliced

8 oz/225 g smoked salmon, cut into bite-size pieces

finely grated peel of ½ lemon

pepper

2 tbsp chopped fresh chives

Smoked Salmon, Sour Cream, and Mustard Sauce

Once an expensive luxury, smoked salmon is now more affordable as a result of fish farming. Even so, it is still something of a treat. Some stores sell inexpensive trimmings, the slightly misshapen pieces left over after the salmon has been sliced. These taste just as good and as the fish needs to be cut into bite-size pieces in this recipe, will not affect the appearance.

• Cook the pasta in plenty of boiling salted water until al dente. Drain and return to the pan. Add the sour cream, mustard, scallions, smoked salmon, and lemon peel to the pasta. Stir over a low heat until heated through. Season with pepper.

• Transfer to a serving dish. Sprinkle with the chives. Serve warm or at room temperature.

Asparagus with Hollandaise Sauce

SERVES 4

1 lb 7 oz/650 g white or green asparagus

HOLLANDAISE SAUCE

4 tbsp white wine vinegar

½ tbsp finely chopped shallot

5 black peppercorns

1 bay leaf

3 large egg yolks

1¼ sticks unsalted butter, finely diced

2 tsp lemon juice

pinch of cayenne pepper

2 tbsp light cream (optional)

salt

In France the whole country celebrates when asparagus comes into season in April. It features on menus du jour from cafes to Michelin-starred restaurants. Market stalls pile it high and roadside stalls sell it at farm gates.

• Whether you are using white or green asparagus, break off any woody ends of the stems. Trim the stalks so that they are all the same height. Use a small knife or vegetable peeler to remove the stringy fibers from the white asparagus, trimming from the tip towards the end.

• Bring a kettle of water to a boil. Divide the asparagus into 4 bundles and use kitchen string to tie the bundles together, criss-crossing the string from just below the tips to the base so that the bundles can stand upright.

• Stand the bundles upright in the deepest pan you have. Pour in enough water to come about three-quarters of the way up the stalks and then cover them with a loose tent of foil, shiny-side down, inside the pan.

• Heat the water in the pan until bubbles appear around the side of the pan, then continue simmering for 10 minutes, or until the stalks are just tender when pierced with the tip of a knife.

• Meanwhile, to make the Hollandaise Sauce, put the vinegar, shallot, peppercorns, and bay leaf in a small pan over high heat and boil until reduced to 1 tablespoon. Let cool slightly, then strain into a heatproof bowl that will fit over a pan of simmering water without the bowl touching the water.

• Beat the egg yolks into the reduced vinegar mixture. Set the bowl over the pan of simmering water and whisk the egg yolks constantly until the yolks are thick enough to leave a trail on the surface. Do not let the water boil.

• Gradually beat in the pieces of butter, piece by piece, whisking constantly until the sauce is like soft mayonnaise. Stir in the lemon juice, then add salt to taste and the cayenne pepper. Stir in the cream for a richer taste, if desired. Transfer to 4 small serving bowls.

• Drain the asparagus well. Untie the bundles and arrange the spears on individual plates. Serve immediately with the bowls of Hollandaise Sauce. To eat, pick up the asparagus, stalk by stalk, and dip the tips in the hot sauce.

EARL GUILLEMET
Route de Fontainebleau
Tél:01 64 98 85 97

MAKES ABOUT 3 CUPS

4 tbsp olive oil
10 large garlic cloves
5 oz/140 g shallots, chopped
4 large red bell peppers, cored, seeded, and chopped
2 lb 4 oz/1 kg good-flavored ripe, fresh tomatoes, chopped, or 2 lb 12 oz/1.25 kg good-quality canned chopped tomatoes
2 thin strips freshly pared orange rind
pinch hot red pepper flakes (optional), to taste
salt and pepper

Tomato and Bell Pepper Sauce

The amount of orange rind you add to this simple, all-purpose sauce really changes its character. Large strips of rind, for example, lift the flavors in winter when fresh tomatoes are insipid.

• Heat the olive oil in a large, flameproof casserole over medium heat. Add the garlic, shallots, and bell peppers and cook for 10 minutes, stirring occasionally, until the bell peppers are soft, but not brown.

• Add the tomatoes, including the juices if using canned ones, orange rind, hot pepper flakes, if using, and salt and pepper to taste and bring to a boil. Reduce the heat to as low as possible and let simmer, uncovered, for 45 minutes, or until the liquid evaporates and the sauce thickens.

• Purée the sauce through a mouli. Alternatively, purée in a food processor, then use a wooden spoon to press through a fine strainer. Taste and adjust the seasoning if necessary. Use at once, or cover and chill for up to 3 days.

SERVES 4–6

generous 1/3 cup sea salt

24 small, new red-skinned potatoes, unpeeled and kept whole

MOJO SAUCE

1½ oz/40 g day-old bread, crusts removed and torn into small pieces

2 large garlic cloves

½ tsp salt

1½ tbsp hot Spanish paprika

1 tbsp ground cumin

about 2 tbsp red wine vinegar

about 5 tbsp extra-virgin olive oil

2 pimientos del piquillo, preserved, drained

Wrinkled Potatoes with Mojo Sauce

Have plenty of cold beers or water on hand when you serve this classic tapas. The potatoes are cooked in heavily salted water to resemble seawater, resulting in a thin film of salt on the skins. The salt and piquant sauce are very thirst making.

• Pour about 1 inch/2.5 cm water in a pan and stir in the sea salt. Add the potatoes and stir again; they do not have to be covered with water. Fold a clean dish towel to fit over the potatoes, then bring the water to a boil. Reduce the heat and let simmer for 20 minutes, or until the potatoes are tender but still holding together.

• Remove the dish towel and set aside. Drain the potatoes and return them to the empty pan. When the dish towel is cool enough to handle, wring the saltwater it contains into the pan. Put the pan over low heat and shake until the potatoes are dry and coated with a thin white film. Remove from the heat.

• Meanwhile, make the Mojo Sauce. Put the bread in a bowl and add just enough water to cover, set aside for 5 minutes to soften. Use your hands to squeeze all the water from the bread. Use a mortar and pestle to mash the garlic and salt into a paste. Stir in the paprika and cumin. Transfer the mixture to a food processor. Add 2 tablespoons of vinegar and blend, then add the bread and 2 tablespoons of oil and blend again.

• With the motor running, add the pepper pieces a few at a time until they are puréed and a sauce forms. Add more oil, if necessary, until the sauce is smooth and thick. Taste and adjust the seasoning, adding extra vinegar, if necessary.

• To serve, cut the potatoes in half and spear with wooden toothpicks. Serve with a bowl of sauce on the side for dipping. The potatoes can be eaten hot or at room temperature.

SERVES 4

3 tbsp olive oil
3 tbsp butter
4 garlic cloves, chopped very finely
2 tbsp finely diced red bell pepper
2 tbsp tomato paste
½ cup dry white wine
1 lb/450 g tagliatelle or spaghetti
12 oz/350 g raw shrimp, shelled, cut into ½ inch/1 cm pieces
½ cup heavy cream
salt and pepper
3 tbsp chopped fresh flat-leaf parsley, to garnish

Shrimp and Garlic Sauce with Cream

It is best to remove the black vein that runs along the back of the shrimp. Make a shallow cut with a sharp knife along the length of the peeled shrimp and remove the vein with the tip of the knife or the point of a toothpick. While it is not toxic, the thread-like vein can adversely affect the flavor of the dish.

• Heat the oil and butter in a pan over a medium–low heat. Add the garlic and red bell pepper. Cook for a few seconds, or until the garlic is just beginning to color. Stir in the tomato paste and the wine, and cook for 10 minutes, stirring.

• Cook the pasta in plenty of boiling salted water until al dente. Drain and return to the pan.

• Add the shrimp to the sauce and raise the heat to medium–high. Cook for 2 minutes, stirring, until the shrimp turn pink. Reduce the heat and stir in the cream. Cook for 1 minute, stirring constantly, until thickened. Season with salt and pepper.

• Transfer the pasta to a warm serving dish. Pour the sauce over the pasta. Sprinkle with the parsley. Toss well to mix and serve at once.

In this section you will find the most useful sauces and dressings for all occasions. We have become used to buying many of these basics at the supermarket so tasting the homemade versions for the first time is likely to prove a revelation. For a start, using fresh ingredients makes a huge difference and the absence of any artificial additives is reassuring for the health-conscious. Also, it's simple to make slight adjustments so that the flavor and texture are precisely to your liking. Many of these recipes are immensely versatile and form the basis of a wide variety of other sauces and dressings, which simply require the addition of an extra ingredient or two, whether fresh herbs or chopped anchovy fillets. Finally, the recipe for Mayonnaise should at last dispel the misbegotten notion that there is something incredibly difficult about making this useful, popular—and easy—cold sauce.

ESSENTIAL RECIPES

SERVES 2–4

2 tbsp lemon juice, or red or white wine vinegar

4–6 tbsp extra-virgin olive oil

1 tsp Dijon mustard

pinch of superfine sugar

1 tbsp chopped fresh parsley

salt and pepper

Basic Dressings

A basic dressing is essential for a good salad. Good olive oil and a fine vinegar or lemon juice should be used. Vary the oil and vinegar according to the salad ingredients and add appropriate herbs at the last minute. Salads should only be dressed immediately before eating or else the greens will go soggy. For the simplest dressing, just sprinkle on some freshly squeezed lemon juice and some olive oil.

• Place all the ingredients in a jar, secure the top, and shake well. Alternatively, beat all the ingredients together in a small bowl. Use as much oil as you like. If you have just salad greens to dress, then 4 tablespoons of oil will be sufficient, but if you have heavier ingredients like potatoes, you will need 6 tablespoons of oil.

• Use the dressing at once. If you want to store it, do not add the herbs—it will then keep for 3–4 days in the refrigerator.

Variations

ASIAN DRESSING: replace 1 tablespoon of the oil with sesame oil and add 1–2 teaspoons of soy sauce. Add chopped cilantro instead of the parsley.

TOMATO DRESSING: use balsamic vinegar instead of lemon juice and add 1 tablespoon of chopped sun-dried tomatoes. Replace the parsley with torn basil leaves.

CHEESE DRESSING: add 1 tablespoon of crumbled strong blue cheese, or fork in 1 tablespoon of garlic-flavored soft cheese. A few chopped walnuts, say ¼ cup, would be a nice addition.

SWEET-AND-SOUR DRESSING: add 1 tablespoon of honey and 1 teaspoon finely grated fresh gingerroot. Some toasted sesame seeds, about 1 tablespoon, would add a good crunch.

MAKES ABOUT 2/3 CUP

1/2 cup olive or other vegetable oil

3 tbsp white wine vinegar or lemon juice

1 tsp Dijon mustard

1/2 tsp superfine sugar

salt and pepper

Vinaigrette

This dressing is a great way to capture the flavor of simple salads, and with so few ingredients, it is essential to use good-quality oil and vinegar.

• Put all the ingredients in a jar, then use a stick blender to blend until a thick emulsion forms. Alternatively, put all the ingredients in a screw-top jar, then secure the lid and shake well until the emulsion forms. Taste, and adjust the seasoning if necessary.

• Use at once or store in an airtight container in the refrigerator for up to a month. Always whisk or shake the dressing again before using.

Variations

GARLIC VINAIGRETTE: Use a good-quality garlic-flavored oil and add 1 or 2 crushed garlic cloves to taste. The longer the garlic cloves are left in the dressing, the more pronounced the flavor will be, but they should be removed after a week.

HERB VINAIGRETTE: Stir 1 1/2 tablespoons chopped fresh herbs, such as chives, parsley, or mint, or a mixture, into the basic vinaigrette. Use within 3 days and strain through a fine non-metallic strainer if the herbs start to darken.

MAKES ABOUT 1¼ CUPS

2 large egg yolks
2 tsp Dijon mustard
¾ tsp salt, or to taste
2 tbsp lemon juice or white wine vinegar
about 1¼ cups sunflower-seed oil
white pepper

Mayonnaise

One of the basic sauces in the French repertoire, home-made mayonnaise has a milder flavor than most commercial varieties.

• Whiz the egg yolks with the Dijon mustard, salt, and white pepper to taste in a food processor or blender or by hand. Add the lemon juice and whiz again.

• With the motor still running or still beating, add the oil, drop by drop at first. When the sauce begins to thicken, add the oil in a slow, steady stream. Taste and adjust the seasoning with extra salt, pepper, and lemon juice, if necessary. If the sauce seems too thick, slowly add 1 tablespoon hot water, light cream, or lemon juice.

• Use at once or store in an airtight container in the refrigerator for up to 1 week.

MAKES ABOUT 1½ CUPS

- 1 large mango, about 14 oz/400 g, peeled, pitted, and finely chopped
- 2 tbsp lime juice
- 1 tbsp vegetable or peanut oil
- 2 shallots, finely chopped
- 1 garlic clove, finely chopped
- 2 fresh green chilies, seeded and finely sliced
- 1 tsp black mustard seeds
- 1 tsp coriander seeds
- 5 tbsp grated jaggery or brown sugar
- 5 tbsp white wine vinegar
- 1 tsp salt
- pinch of ground ginger

Mango Chutney

This light, spiced chutney is about as far as one can get from the thick, overly sweet mango chutney that can be bought in jars. It adds a sunny flavor to any meal.

• Put the mango in a nonmetallic bowl with the lime juice and set aside.

• Heat the oil in a large skillet or pan over medium-high heat. Add the shallots and sauté for 3 minutes. Add the garlic and chilies and stir for an additional 2 minutes, or until the shallots are soft, but not brown. Add the mustard and coriander seeds, then stir around.

• Add the mango to the pan with the jaggery, vinegar, salt, and ginger and stir around. Reduce the heat to its lowest setting and simmer for 10 minutes until the liquid thickens and the mango becomes sticky.

• Remove from the heat and let cool completely. Transfer to an airtight container, cover, and chill for 3 days before using. Store in the refrigerator and use within 1 week.

SERVES 6–8

BREAD SAUCE
1 onion
12 cloves
1 bay leaf
6 black peppercorns
2½ cups milk
2 cups fresh white bread crumbs
2 tbsp butter
whole nutmeg, for grating
2 tbsp heavy cream, optional
salt and pepper

CRANBERRY SAUCE
2 cups fresh cranberries
6 tbsp soft brown sugar
2/3 cup orange juice
½ tsp ground cinnamon
½ tsp grated nutmeg

Bread and Cranberry Sauces

Bread sauce is a traditional accompaniment to turkey for Christmas, but is also very useful for serving with cold meats, such as chicken or ham.

- To make bread sauce make small holes in the onion using the point of a sharp knife or a skewer, and stick the cloves in them.
- Put the onion, bay leaf, and peppercorns in a pan and pour in the milk. Bring to a boil, then remove from the heat, cover, and leave to steep for 1 hour.
- To make the sauce, discard the onion and bay leaf, and strain the milk to remove the peppercorns. Return the milk to the cleaned pan and add the bread crumbs.
- Cook the sauce over very low heat for 4–5 minutes until the bread crumbs have swollen and the sauce is thick.
- Beat in the butter and season well with the salt and pepper, and a good grating of nutmeg. Stir in the cream just before serving, if using.
- To make the cranberry sauce place the cranberries, sugar, orange juice, and spices in a pan and stir well. Cover the pan and bring slowly to a boil over gentle heat.
- Simmer for 8–10 minutes until the cranberries have burst. Take care because they may splash.
- Put the sauce in a serving bowl and cover until needed. Serve warm or cold.

SERVES 6

APRICOT SAUCE

14 oz/400 g canned apricot halves in syrup

2/3 cup vegetable stock (made from powder)

½ cup Marsala wine

½ tsp ground ginger

½ tsp ground cinnamon

salt and pepper

HORSERADISH SAUCE

6 tbsp creamed horseradish sauce

6 tbsp crème fraîche

MINT SAUCE

small bunch fresh mint leaves

2 tsp superfine sugar

2 tbsp boiling water

2 tbsp white wine vinegar

Apricot, Mint, and Horseradish Sauces

The recipe listed here for mint sauce is a simple classic—you can vary it by experimenting with different vinegars, for example malt vinegar, cider vinegar, or tarragon wine vinegar, among others. Mint sauce is so versatile, you can even add extra ingredients like honey.

• For the apricot sauce, put the canned apricots and syrup into a blender and blend until smooth.

• Pour the pureé into a pan, add the other ingredients, and mix well. Heat the sauce gently over low heat for about 4–5 minutes until warm. Season to taste.

• Remove from the heat and pour into a serving pitcher. This sauce goes well with cured ham.

• For the horseradish sauce, mix the horseradish and crème fraîche together in a small serving bowl. Serve the sauce with roast beef or smoked fish, such as trout or mackerel.

• For the mint sauce, make sure the mint is clean and tear the leaves from their stems. If the mint is dirty, wash it gently and dry thoroughly before tearing. place the leaves on the cutting board and sprinkle with the sugar. Chop the leaves finely (the sugar helps the chopping process) and place in a small bowl. Pour in the boiling water and stir to dissolve the sugar.

• Add the vinegar and let stand for 30 minutes. This sauce goes particularly well with roast lamb.

Sometimes, especially for everyday family meals, dessert is a bit of an afterthought and something of a poor relation to the main course. The sweet sauces in this section provide an easy way to turn a simple dessert into a triumphant finale to family supper. All of them, hot and cold, will transform a scoop of ready-made ice cream, but they also go well with a huge range of other sweet treats from steamed puddings to pancakes and from tarts to mousses. Just because they're easy to make doesn't mean that they aren't good enough to serve to guests—any of the Ice Cream Sauces would go beautifully with a meringue gateau and Chocolate Fudge Sauce is just perfect for a fruit-packed, nut-sprinkled ice cream sundae. For adult guests only, a fresh fruit fondue with French Chocolate Sauce would be a fabulous end to an al fresco meal.

SWEET SAUCES

MAKES SCANT 1 CUP

2/3 cup heavy cream

4 tbsp butter, sweet for preference, cut into small pieces

3 tbsp superfine sugar

6 oz/175 g white chocolate, broken into pieces

2 tbsp cognac

Chocolate Fudge Sauce

This creamy white chocolate sauce adds a touch of sophistication and luxury to the dinner table.

• Pour the cream into the top of a double boiler or a heatproof bowl set over a pan of barely simmering water. Add the butter and sugar and stir until the mixture is smooth. Remove from the heat.

• Stir in the chocolate, a few pieces at a time, waiting until each batch has melted before adding the next. Add the cognac and stir the sauce until smooth. Cool to room temperature before serving.

MAKES 2/3 CUP

6 tbsp heavy cream

3 oz/85 g semisweet chocolate, broken into small pieces

2 tbsp orange-flavored liqueur

French Chocolate Sauce

This rich, warm and alcoholic sauce is superb with both hot and cold desserts and positively magical with ice cream.

• Bring the cream gently to a boil in a small, heavy based pan over low heat. Remove the pan from the heat, add the chocolate and stir until smooth.

• Stir in the liqueur and serve immediately, or keep the sauce warm until required.

SERVES 6

BERRY SAUCE

- scant 1 cup berries, such as blackberries or raspberries
- 2 tbsp water
- 2–3 tbsp superfine sugar
- 2 tbsp fruit liqueur, such as cassis or raspberry-flavored liqueur

MOCHA SAUCE

- 2/3 cup heavy cream
- 4 tbsp butter, sweet for preference
- 2 oz/55 g light muscovado sugar
- scant 1 cup semisweet chocolate, broken into pieces
- 2 tbsp dark rum (optional)

PORT SAUCE

- 1½ cups ruby port
- 2 tsp cornstarch

Berry, Mocha, and Port Ice Cream Sauces

Serve plain or chocolate ice cream with one or more of these delicious sauces on the side.

• For the berry sauce, put all the ingredients into a small, heavy-based pan and heat gently, until the sugar has dissolved and the fruit juices run. Purée with a hand-held blender or in a food processor, then push through a strainer into a serving bowl to remove the seeds. Add more sugar if necessary and serve warm or cold.

• For the mocha sauce, pour the cream in a heatproof bowl and add the butter and sugar. Set over a pan of gently simmering water and cook, stirring constantly, until smooth. Remove from the heat and set aside to cool slightly.

• Stir in the chocolate and continue stirring until it has melted. Stir in the rum (if using), then leave the sauce to cool to room temperature before serving.

• For the port sauce, combine 1/4 cup of the port with the cornstarch to make a smooth paste. Pour the remainder of the port into a pan and bring to a boil. Stir in the cornstarch paste and cook, stirring constantly, for about 1 minute, until thickened. Remove from the heat and set aside to cool. Pour into a bowl, cover, and chill in the refrigerator.

Index